GHOSTS
Bandits & Legends
Of Old Monterey,
Carmel, and Surrounding Areas

GHOSTS
Bandits & Legends
Of Old Monterey, Carmel, and Surrounding Areas

Randall A. Reinstedt

Illustrated by
Ed Greco and Thornton Harby

Ghost Town Publications
Carmel, California

If bookstores in your area do not carry *Ghosts, Bandits and Legends of Old Monterey,* copies may be obtained by writing to . . .

GHOST TOWN PUBLICATIONS
P.O. Drawer 5998
Carmel, CA 93921

For other books by Randall A. Reinstedt see page 87.

This book is a revised and expanded version of the work by the same title published in 1974.

10 9 8 7 6 5 4

Manufactured in the United States of America

Library of Congress Catalog Number 74-189524
ISBN 0-933818-00-9

Edited by John Bergez
Typesetting and design by Erick and Mary Ann Reinstedt

This book is dedicated to the people of the Monterey Peninsula . . . who have lived the legends, and, in sharing their stories, kept the legends alive

MONTEREY
PENINSULA

POINT
PINOS

PACIFIC
GROVE

POINT
CABRILLO

POINT JOE

MONTEREY

**MONTEREY
BAY**

**PACIFIC
OCEAN**

CYPRESS
POINT

PEBBLE
BEACH

PESCADERO
POINT

CARMEL

**CARMEL
BAY**

CALIFORNIA

POINT
LOBOS

N

**CARMEL
HIGHLANDS**

TO MASSACRE CAVE AND THE
LOS BURROS MINING DISTRICT

Contents

Acknowledgments

It would be difficult to list all of the people who have graciously given of their time to help make this book possible. In an attempt to recognize a chosen few, I would like to single out Barbara Burdick and the late Harry Downie. Barbara has worked at several of Monterey's aged adobes and is extremely knowledge able about them. Without her willingness to share this knowledge, and some of her past experiences, a number of the stories related in this work—particularly those about the Robert Louis Stevenson House—would have had to remain unrecorded.

Before his death in 1980, Harry Downie was recognized as California's leading authority on mission restoration. Among his many masterpieces is the beautifully restored Mission San Carlos Borromeo del Rio Carmelo (Carmel Mission). As with Barbara, without Harry's wonderful memory, and his willingness to share some of his special stories, certain tales contained in these pages would have remained untold.

Among the other individuals who played important parts in the original writing of this work are Lee Harbick, Jessie Sandholdt, and Bill Martin (now deceased). As in the book's first printing, I would like to thank these people for their help, interest, and encouragement.

Numerous old-timers, countless volumes of Monterey history, and several early copies of the *Monterey Peninsula Herald* (as well as other early local newspapers) were consulted in the preparation of this work. With this in mind, I would like to thank

the old-timers, and the staffs of the Peninsula's many fine librar-
ies, for making their sources available to me.

Finally, I am grateful to Debbie, Erick, and Mary Ann (the
rest of the Reinstedts) for their understanding and help in making
this updated and expanded edition possible.

Introduction

Perhaps it should come as no surprise that spirits of bygone eras are said to frequent many of the aged buildings of Monterey and transmit feelings of presence to those who explore their gardens and walk their hallways. After all, Monterey boasts a history that dates back more than two centuries and includes such colorful and important events as being the capital under both Spanish and Mexican rule; surviving a frightful siege by the dreaded privateer Hippolyte Bouchard; experiencing a premature invasion by overeager American forces; serving as the site of California's blustery Constitutional Convention; giving birth to the infamous outlaw Tiburcio Vasquez; being home for a brief time to the wayworn writer Robert Louis Stevenson (and, at a later date, to prize-winning author John Steinbeck); becoming the destination of travelers from throughout the land with the opening of the fabulous Hotel Del Monte in 1880; and, not to be forgotten, being internationally known as the Sardine Capital of the World and the site of Steinbeck's famed Cannery Row. Any place so rich in historic personalities and events must have its share of unwritten history, tales, and mysteries—and Monterey is certainly no exception.

As many California history buffs know, in days of old Monterey was often thought of as being synonymous with the areas that now include Pacific Grove, Pebble Beach, and Carmel. Today it is these communities that make up the beautiful Monterey Peninsula. And, it is the ghosts, bandits, and legends of these same communities—with additional tales from Carmel Valley, Point Lobos, Carmel Highlands, the Santa Lucia Mountains, and the fog-plagued waters of the Pacific Ocean—that this book is about.

All of these places boast intriguing tales of days gone by—accounts that are interspersed with stories of haunted buildings, ghostly spirits, lost treasures, feared bandits, strange happenings, legendary sea monsters, and unsolved mysteries.

In this book I share a few of these early accounts and introduce you to some of the legends and lore that help to make the Monterey area so special. I hope that these stories will whet your imagination and encourage you to learn more about California's first capital city and its surrounding areas.

About This Revised Edition

This book began as the outgrowth of a magazine article I wrote for a Monterey Peninsula publication in 1970, Monterey's bicentennial year. The two-part article, called "Ghosts of Old Monterey," created so much interest that I chose to follow it up with a small book of the same name. Popular among the locals, the first and only printing of the book soon sold out. Buoyed by the book's success, I decided to expand it and add some information about treasures and bandits, as well as an assortment of other local legends.

Published in 1972, the book was called *Ghosts, Bandits and Legends of Old Monterey*. Enthusiastically received by both residents and visitors, the book has enjoyed a long shelf life, having been reprinted ten times and having sold more than 30,000 copies on the Monterey Peninsula alone.

Since the publication of *Ghosts, Bandits and Legends*, I have kept busy writing other books about the Monterey Bay area (frequently referred to as my Paperback Series) as well as a children's history series (called Randall A. Reinstedt's History and Happenings of California Series). Books in both series tell about people, places, and interesting events that have taken place in California, including information about gold mines, treasures, pirates, shipwrecks, sea monsters, Monterey's famed fishing industry . . . and more ghosts! (In fact, five of the ten books that make up the Paperback Series are about ghosts.)

This brings me back to *Ghosts, Bandits and Legends* and this revision. With the book having been in print for more than twenty years, and with my continued research into old Monterey and its environs, it is only natural that I would come up with other tales about this history-rich area. Of course, many of these accounts have been incorporated into my other books. Because I didn't want to repeat these accounts when I began the task of updating and expanding this publication, I concentrated on adding to the existing tales (when, and if, information had come to light since the original text was recorded) and including new stories that fit the subject matter of this book (such as the fascinating account of Joaquin Murrieta—one of the West's most notorious badmen—returning to Carmel Valley *after* he was supposedly beheaded by the California Rangers!).

Because I have generally avoided repeating stories and details that I have since written about in other works, interested readers may want to seek out my other books for elaborations and embellishments of many of the tales recounted in these pages (see page 87 for a list). From time to time I refer to these related accounts when they are especially pertinent. But whether or not your exploration extends beyond this book, I'm sure you will find that ghosts, bandits, and legends add even more color and drama to the fascinating story of California's first capital city.

Chapter One

Monterey's Robert Louis Stevenson House

Probably one of the best-known ghosts on the California coast is the Lady in Black who frequents Monterey's popular Robert Louis Stevenson House. This aged adobe was built in the 1830s, and it was here that Stevenson lived for a brief period in 1879. (Today the Stevenson House is part of the California State Park system. It is open to the public on a guided-tour basis and is located at 530 Houston Street.)

The Lady in Black is thought by many to be the spirit of Mrs. Juan Girardin, who owned the building at the time Stevenson stayed there. The structure was then known as the French Hotel.

Other staunch Stevensonites claim that the mysterious lady is the ghost of Fanny Osbourne, the woman Stevenson had come all the way from Scotland to be near. They back up their claim with heartwarming stories of Mrs. Osbourne's spirit returning to the house to be near Stevenson during his period of ill health. It is true that the young writer was in poor health while he was in Monterey, but history tells us that Jules Simoneau—a Frenchman who owned a nearby restaurant, and who became a lifelong friend of Stevenson—did more to help him through this difficult time than the lady who eventually became his wife.

Those who believe the ghost to be that of Mrs. Girardin point to the year Stevenson lodged at the house as ample reason for her troubled spirit to return. That year, 1879, was a time of hardship and anguish for Manuela Girardin. In the summer her husband died, and in December her grandchildren are said to have become gravely ill, perhaps as a result of a fever epidemic that spread through Monterey County.

Proponents of the Girardin theory also point to a significant sighting of the Lady in Black by the guide/curator of the Stevenson Memorial. Late one afternoon the guide was somewhat absent-mindedly going about her duties, checking each room prior to locking up for the night. Lost in her own thoughts as she made the rounds, she was suddenly taken aback when she reached the children's nursery and saw a woman—costumed in black—standing near the foot of the bed. Located at the far (south) end of the upstairs hall, the nursery is reminiscent of an old-fashioned children's room. Period furnishings, combined with antique dolls and toys of other kinds, help to give the room a look of the late 1800s. In 1970, when this incident took place, there were steel bars at the entrance to the nursery (as well as some of the other upstairs rooms) to prevent people from damaging or stealing the objects that were inside.

Listening politely, the Lady in Black nodded and smiled warmly when the guide told her it was closing time and she would have to leave.

About to continue her rounds, the guide suddenly realized that no one had entered the building in costume and, even if anyone had, it would have been impossible for a visitor to slip between the narrow steel bars at the entrance to the room. Turning about quickly, she saw that the nursery was empty!

On reflection, the guide believes that what she saw on that cold, foggy day was the ghost of Mrs. Girardin, who had returned

. . . she was suddenly taken aback when she reached the children's nursery and saw a woman—costumed in black—standing near the foot of the bed.

to the nursery to watch over her two sick grandchildren in their time of need. She still has a vivid memory of this lonely lady, dressed in an ankle-length dress complete with a high, black-lace collar, gazing reflectively at the children's empty bed.

A second well-known nursery happening also involves one of the Stevenson House guides. One miserable day in Monterey, when it was much too cold and wet for people to tour old buildings, the bored guide was counting the minutes until she could close. Wandering through the empty house to help pass the time, she stopped at the entrance of the nursery. As she peered between the bars, her attention focused on a wooden Noah's Ark and its collection of animals scattered about the floor near a corner of the room. (The ark and its animals are said to have been made in Germany in the mid-1800s.) Deciding to examine the toys more closely, she opened the cell-like door and made herself comfortable on the floor. After admiring the workmanship of each piece, she took the time to put the creatures in pairs and place them on a ramp leading to the ark. When five o'clock arrived she locked the nursery door and checked the rest of the structure before going on her way.

The next day dawned bright and cheerful. As the guide unlocked the Stevenson Memorial, she was anxious to peek into the nursery to see how the ark and its collection of creatures looked with the morning sun streaming in the windows.

Moments later she arrived at the nursery entrance and peered between the bars. Much to her dismay, the place where she had left the toys was empty. Neither the ark nor its animals could be seen!

Shocked by their disappearance, the guide immediately glanced around the rest of the room. To her amazement, on the floor near the foot of the bed was the ark—and next to it was a miniature corral, in which all of the animals she had carefully arranged in pairs were grouped together! A quick check of the facility—including the silent alarm system—proved that no one had been in the building during the night.

Another nursery happening involved the caretaker/gardener of the Stevenson House. He told of checking the structure late one afternoon, prior to locking up for the night, and seeing a large doll in its customary place on the floor of the nursery. Being the first one at the facility the next morning, he again checked the building. Upon reaching the nursery he noticed that the doll was not where it had been the night before. Like the guide in the preceding account, he immediately glanced about the room. To his surprise he saw the doll tucked in a baby's crib! As in the previous tale, no one had been in the building between the caretaker's visits to the nursery.

Another interesting account was also related by the caretaker of this aged adobe. One afternoon after the house had been closed for the day, he was working in the rear gardens when he heard the sounds of a woman singing coming from one of the upstairs rooms. After turning off the alarm, he unlocked the building and checked every room. Not finding anyone, he wondered whether he had been hearing things.

Somewhat puzzled, he locked the facility and returned to the garden, only to hear the woman's voice again! This time the bewildered caretaker summoned the ranger in residence. (The ranger and his family lived in a portion of the Stevenson House that adjoins the main structure.) Together the two men stood outside the house and listened. Soon the ranger also heard a woman singing, "sort of an early ballad, something like a folk song."

Again the alarms were turned off and the building was searched. As before, the structure proved to be void of visitors.

I might interject at this point that the caretaker was by no means a simple or credulous individual. Not only was he highly intelligent, and something of an authority on old Monterey, but rumor has it that he had retired from a very responsible position and worked at the Stevenson House more as a hobby than a job. Sadly, this remarkable man is now deceased.

11

Was the singing woman the Lady in Black? And was it she who moved the toys in the nursery on at least two occasions? There is no way to tell, but two past guides at the Stevenson Memorial are of the opinion that the house is (or was) called home by more than one ghost. On different occasions, many years apart, the sudden rumble of something being moved could be heard throughout the building. Upon checking to see what the commotion was all about, the guides (who were alone at the facility) found that a large wooden trunk in the upstairs sunroom had been moved from its customary location near the east wall to a spot directly across the room and in front of the fireplace. The scratched and marked floor was ample proof that it had been dragged.

Interestingly, both of the guides were women, and both expressed the opinion that the trunk was too heavy to have been moved by a woman.

Visitors to the house, many of whom who are unfamiliar with its past, also report feelings of presence or other unexplainable sensations as they stroll about the building. One pair of ladies even indicated that when they were in the Stevenson bedroom they were overwhelmed by the smell of carbolic acid. I found their account of special interest, as in days of old carbolic acid was often used in a sickroom as a disinfectant—and Robert Louis Stevenson was known to have been ill while he was staying at the structure!* (Incidentally, the Stevenson bedroom contains several items that belonged to the acclaimed writer, including the desk he is thought to have worked at when he wrote *Treasure Island.*)

Another happening involving the Stevenson bedroom fits in nicely at this point. According to this account, one summer day a couple approached the guide's desk. The wife had a strange

---

*Coincidentally, I met one of the ladies who was involved in this incident seventeen years after I first heard the tale from the Stevenson House guide. For a more complete account of the carbolic acid incident, see the tale entitled "It took their breath away . . . " in *Ghost Notes.*

. . . when they were in the Stevenson bedroom they were overwhelmed by the smell of carbolic acid.

request: could the guide accompany her to the Stevenson bedroom? Since it was a slow day for visitors, the guide agreed and followed her to the main staircase. Here the woman turned to her husband and insisted that he remain downstairs. Upon reaching the bedroom, she pointed to a rocking chair and asked, "What makes it move?"

Reaching out and stopping the gently rocking chair, the guide told the woman some of the ghost stories connected with the house. Upon hearing the tales, the woman was speechless. Her husband had first pointed out the moving chair, and she had insisted that he had given it a push. When he denied even having

13

been near the chair, she had marched off to get the guide and prove him wrong. Now that she had heard the tales of the Stevenson House ghost, she decided her husband had been telling the truth. With a last uneasy glance at the rocking chair, she hurried off to beg his forgiveness.

In addition to toys, trunks, and chairs, many other objects in the grand old building are also said to be in a constant state of flux. Some of the items merely move from spot to spot within one room, while others take more extensive trips. Books in Stevenson's bedroom are one example. At times, when certain volumes have been removed from their customary places for purposes of display, they have been found the next day back in their places and in their proper order!

The stereopticon in the upstairs front parlor also has a history of moving. Like the nursery, the parlor had bars at its door when the occurrences took place. The usual location of the stereopticon was near the fireplace, where it could be viewed by visitors. However, on more than one occasion it was found near a window (perhaps to provide better light for its pictures). After this incident was repeated several times, the stereopticon was left on the floor, near the window, in an effort to please the spirits. Unfortunately, when it was near the window it was almost out of sight of the building's visitors.

Also a part of the "moving game" was a wine glass in the upstairs back parlor that disappeared from its glass-encased cabinet—only to reappear in its original location several days later. In the adjoining sunroom, a wardrobe closet door has a habit of opening after it has been securely fastened by the conscientious caretaker.

Such incidents may seem harmless enough—unless they happen close to home. One family that used to live in the ranger's quarters decided to move from the building because of several unexplained happenings at the Stevenson Memorial. A partial listing includes door latches rattling in the dead of night, un-

14

earthly noises repeatedly being heard, and the tantalizing aroma of freshly brewed coffee in the wee hours of the morning.

Numerous other tales can be told of unexplainable happenings, but probably the most mysterious—and certainly among the most fascinating—are two incidents that took place during Monterey's Bicentennial Celebration in the summer of 1970.

The first of these tales is about an innocent-appearing rose that was found on a chair in an upstairs bedroom. The rose—fresh and dewy, and unlike the roses in the well-tended gardens below—had been placed in the room sometime during the night or early morning. During that time the house had been locked with all alarms set, proof that no one had been in the building.

Local residents wonder aloud whether the cheery yellow rose was placed there by the Lady in Black and, if so, what special occasion she was honoring.

The second story concerns an authority on tales of the supernatural who requested permission to leave a handwritten manuscript in one of the locked rooms. Permission was granted, and a large manila envelope containing the document was placed in an upstairs room.

The composition was carefully inspected by the caretaker before being put in the room. After the door was locked, the key—which is said to have been the *only* key to the cell-like door—was placed in a self-addressed envelope and mailed to the caretaker's home. This was on a Thursday. By Saturday the key had arrived and the owner of the manuscript had returned for his document.

After taking the key from the envelope and unlocking the door, both of the men examined the manuscript. They were shocked to discover that the pages had been mixed and the original blue handwriting had been corrected with dark black ink. The blotting and scratching on the paper indicated that the pen that had been used was of the old-fashioned quill variety. There is even a rumor that the dark black ink was similar to that of the late 1800s!

To this day no one knows who—or what—corrected the manuscript, but the fact that it *was* corrected has created renewed interest in tales of old Monterey's Robert Louis Stevenson House!

Author's Note

Since the original story concerning ghostly happenings at the Robert Louis Stevenson House was published in 1970, many changes have been made at the aged adobe. Among other things, furniture has been rearranged, the full-length bars have been removed, and escorted tours have been initiated. In addition, over the years many new sightings of the Lady in Black, as well as numerous odd happenings, have reportedly taken place at the facility.

*After listening to the stories, and discussing many of the ghostly occurrences with the people who experienced them (several of which I have documented in my book **Ghost Notes**), I must admit that, in my opinion, the Robert Louis Stevenson House harbors considerably more than lingering memories and antique furnishings!*

Chapter Two

The Royal Presidio Chapel and Rectory

A second well-known Monterey ghost frequents the Royal Presidio Chapel and its neighboring old rectory. Appropriately, these buildings are located on Church Street, near downtown Monterey. The Royal Presidio Chapel dates back to the late 1700s and is the only original presidio chapel left in California. The rectory is located directly west of the chapel. (There is also a newer rectory building on the east side of the church.) The older structure on the west side of the chapel is said to have been built on top of the original rectory building (which reportedly was destroyed by fire). If this is true, perhaps in some way it helps to explain the unearthly happenings.

The majority of the strange goings-on stem from the old rectory, although unnatural events also take place at the aged church. Among the incidents reported to have occurred in the chapel are footsteps heard when no one is there, bells ringing in the dead of night, books and papers moving of their own accord, and candles floating in the air. On at least one occasion, a spirit is said to have placed its hand on a troubled woman's shoulder!

On at least one occasion, a spirit is said to have placed its hand on a troubled woman's shoulder!

Unlike the Robert Louis Stevenson House ghost—whose identity is the subject of some debate—there is general agreement that the spirit that frequents the chapel, and its old rectory, is that of a local priest who served at the parish from the 1890s to the 1920s.

One reason for this belief can be traced to a housekeeper at the old rectory. According to the story, one evening the housekeeper asked the assembled fathers if the "other priest" was going to stay for dinner. Looking around to see that all were accounted for, the fathers asked which priest she was referring to.

Puzzled by the question, the housekeeper proceeded to describe in great detail the father she had seen in the hall. The priests who had served at the Monterey parish for a number of years were astonished when they heard the vivid description she gave of their long departed brother. Needless to say, an added place setting was *not* included for that evening's meal!

Among other old rectory tales is one that tells of a visiting priest who stopped at the facility before continuing south on a hunting trip. Upon retiring for the night the priest took his things to his room in anticipation of an early departure. Suddenly the calm was shattered by the crash of a gun! Rushing to the visitor's room, the other priests (who lived at the rectory) found their guest with shotgun in hand, staring at the spot at which he had fired.

Upon questioning him they learned that he had been awakened by a strange noise. Thinking he was being robbed, he called out to scare the intruder. When there was no response, he grabbed his gun and fired at the shadowy image on the opposite side of the room.

Subsequent investigation revealed that nothing was missing, nothing was disturbed, and nothing was hit by the well-aimed buckshot!

Additional accounts involving the old rectory tell of books falling from shelves and opening to pages where money has been hidden, doors that mysteriously open and close, and lights that blink on and off. But even these tales pale by comparison with the mystifying event that took place there only a few short years ago.

On a typically foggy Monterey night, a local security officer (and former policeman) and a greatly respected Monterey man (with direct ties to the church) were about to enter the old rectory for a security check. As they neared the building, they became aware of the peculiar actions of the officer's police-trained German shepherd. Apparently the animal had suddenly become "spooked"! Not only was it whimpering and whining, but it had tucked its tail between its legs and was tugging on its choke chain in an effort to get away. This behavior amazed the officer, as in the countless rounds they had made together (checking buildings and other out-of-the-way places), he had never seen the dog react in such a way.

With considerable coaxing, pushing, and prodding, the men were finally able to get the shepherd into the rectory. Curious as to how it would react when they were in the building, they turned their flashlights on the dog as soon as they closed the door. To their amazement, instead of cowering in a corner—or frantically clawing at the door in an effort to get out as they half-expected it to do—the shepherd did just the opposite. With its eyes wide, its ears erect, and the hair on its back standing straight up, the animal growled deep in its throat and stared into the darkness.

Suddenly, the shepherd took a mighty leap. Landing on something the men couldn't see, the dog became locked in combat with the invisible force. As the battle raged, the unseen thing apparently began to get the upper hand, for the shepherd was soon flat on its back. Even though there was no blood or other moisture, it was obvious that the animal was under an intense attack, as signs of both biting and chewing were evident about its neck.

Fortunately the dog refused to give up, and managed to slip out from under its adversary. Trading places with the invisible force, the shepherd began to take control of the fight and tore into its foe with a vengeance. In separate interviews with each witness, both men indicated that at the time the dog was attacking the presence all four of its paws were from six to eight inches off the floor!

Whatever the unseen thing was, it evidently managed to get away and make a beeline for a staircase leading to the second floor. Pulling the choke chain from the officer's hand, the shepherd took off in hot pursuit. Following the animal's progress with the beams of their flashlights, the men watched open-mouthed as the shepherd bounded up the stairs, only to lose its opponent near the top.

To this day it is unknown what the presence was that the animal fought with. Interestingly, however, some old-timers say that the priest whose ghost is said to frequent the chapel and its old rectory was once the proud owner of . . . a dog!

Author's Note

*For those who wish to learn more about the buildings discussed in this chapter, additional accounts are recorded in **Ghost Notes** and in **Ghostly Tales and Mysterious Happenings of Old Monterey**. Those who were fascinated by the "spooked dog" story will be interested in knowing that an expanded version of the tale is recounted in **Ghost Notes** (see "The dog was locked in combat . . ."). Also, for those who wonder about the priest whose ghost is said to frequent the Royal Presidio Chapel and its old rectory, his presence has also apparently been seen in the courtyard of Carmel Mission (see the following **Ghost Notes** accounts: "A long dead priest . . . ," "Brief and to the point . . . ," and "The ghostly image walked through the wall . . ."). Finally, for an incident that may involve the ghost of this very same priest inside the Carmel Mission, see "The mystery of the burning candles . . ." in **Ghost Notes**.*

Chapter Three

More Monterey Haunts

In addition to the Robert Louis Stevenson House and the Royal Presidio Chapel (and its old rectory), Monterey has many other buildings that boast ghostly spirits and intriguing tales. Listed in this chapter are a selected few.

One of Monterey's best known structures is the Custom House. Known today as the Number One State Historical Monument, this facility was built in the 1820s (with additions being made in later years). Located across from the entrance of Fisherman's Wharf, the building is set up today much the way it was when it was a working custom house and Monterey was the only official port of entry along the Alta California coast. It is only fitting that one of the most historic buildings in the western United States should have its share of ghosts.

Among the many accounts relating to this structure are tales recounted by a family of five who lived there prior to the turn of the century. Apparently, several members of this family experienced strange happenings while they were there. One family member described a series of nightly visitations she received from the ghost of a man and a young lad. Upon speaking to her, the man claimed that he and his companion had both been killed in the building and that their bodies had been buried under the floorboards. (The graves were said to be located near the foot of a staircase leading to one of the structure's two towers.) The man requested that their bodies be uncovered and their remains given a proper burial. However, of more interest to the lady—as well as the rest of her family—was a tale the man told about a pot of gold he had hidden in the building. In fact, he stated it was because of the gold that he had been killed!

This story is interesting for many reasons, not the least of which is the missing pot of gold! More fascinating to ghost buffs, however, is an account that was shared with me by a past curator at the facility. The curator said that she got an "eerie feeling" whenever she climbed the stairs to the storehouse, which was located in the structure's south tower. I'll leave it up to you whether there is a connection between these tales, as to the best of my knowledge the curator was unaware of the ghost sto- ries—or of the graves that were concealed under the steps of one of the building's towers.*

The Larkin House gardens are next on our list of Monterey sites with a ghostly past. The Larkin House and its grounds are on the corner of Calle Principal, Jefferson, and Pacific streets. Thomas Oliver Larkin, California's first and only American consul to Mexico, was the man responsible for building the two main structures located on these grounds. Both of the buildings were constructed in the 1830s. The larger of the two structures is known as the Larkin House and is considered an outstanding example of Monterey Colonial architecture. Over the years it has hosted countless social functions, important business meetings, and several early incidents of California intrigue.

The second Larkin-built building in the garden area also boasts an interesting history. One example takes us back to the

*As I indicated earlier, several other ghostly happenings are also said to have been experienced by the family of five. For more information about these people, see the Custom House account in *Ghostly Tales and Mysterious Happenings of Old Monterey.*

24

1840s, when lieutenants William T. Sherman and Henry W. Halleck stayed there. Both of these men went on to become well-known American generals, with Sherman eventually becoming the commanding general of the United States Army. Perhaps it is for this reason that the aged adobe is now known as Sherman's Quarters.

It was in the Larkin House gardens adjoining these two structures that, according to legend, a human skeleton was once found. As word of this gruesome find became known, the story that went with it hinted that the Spanish once used the grounds of the Larkin House to bury murdered political prisoners.

This legend brings us to a second tale involving a body within the Larkin House gardens. According to rumor, many years ago (but long after the Spanish period) a man was murdered on the grounds. The murderers are said to have dumped the body in a well (which is still visible). Those who are aware of the murder speculate that a ghost that has been observed in the Larkin House gardens is the man who was murdered there, and whose body was thrown into the well.

Not far from the Larkin House is Casa Alvarado, located near the corner of Dutra and Jefferson streets. Like the two buildings just discussed, this aged adobe (with its clapboard siding) dates back to the 1830s. The dwelling was built by Juan Bautista Alvarado, the first Monterey-born governor of California.

A somewhat comical story about Alvarado and his problems with a new adornment to his residence flagpole has come down to us from a dusty volume of Monterey history. It seems that early one morning the governor was awakened by his French cook, who was in the front garden jumping wildly up and down and pointing a trembling finger toward the flagpole. Racing from the house, Alvarado joined his chef in the garden. Shielding his eyes from the glare, he stared at the pole and immediately saw what had frightened his cook.

*Perched squarely atop the pole, and gleaming bril-
liantly in the sun, was a polished human skull!*

Perched squarely atop the pole, and gleaming brilliantly in the sun, was a polished human skull! Much to Alvarado's chagrin, his cook—whom he prized as the best chef in all of California—wasn't about to wait around for an explanation. Hurriedly he packed his bags and left.

Alvarado was not one to let an opportunity pass him by. As news of the adornment atop the flagpole spread about the town, he publicly blamed the presence of the skull on his "grave robbing" political foes. Such a crime, he declared, was "too monstrous for a native Californian!"

A stone's throw from Casa Alvarado is beautiful Colton Hall. Located between Madison and Jefferson streets, the hall faces Pacific Street. Completed in the spring of 1849, the edifice was built by convict labor and financed (to a large extent) from taxes on liquor shops and fines from gamblers. Reverend Walter Colton, the first American alcalde (mayor) of Monterey, spearheaded the building of the hall. When it was completed, the structure was considered the "finest and most pretentious" building in all of California. It was here that the California Constitutional Convention was held in the latter part of 1849.

Tradition states that in the years following the convention the lower part of the hall was used as a school, with the upper part being used for public assemblies. Just as today, school holidays were usually looked forward to by students of yore. However, the children who attended the Colton Hall school were often strangely reluctant to leave when an unscheduled holiday was announced. The reason for this sudden interest in their studies, legend states, was that "school was dismissed when there was a prisoner to execute because the porch of Colton Hall made a handy scaffold"!

While there is considerable debate whether anyone was ever hung from the Colton Hall balcony, I would be remiss not to mention that one worker has told me there is a definite ghostly presence about the facility, and that spooky things *do* happen there.

Casa Pacheco, known today as the Pacheco Club, is another building with a colorful past. Situated on the corner of Abrego and Webster streets, the structure was built around 1840 by Don Francisco Pacheco, a wealthy landowner and former soldier. This two-story adobe has served many purposes over the years, including those of a dance hall and hospital. It is now an exclusive luncheon and social club for men.

Perhaps the best-known of the ghostly happenings at Casa Pacheco are the unnerving sounds of glass breaking and of pots and pans being rattled around. The loud noises, which have been heard by several people, always come from the kitchen. When the sounds are investigated, no broken glass can be found, and not a pot or pan is out of place. No one knows what causes the noises—or who cleans up the mess!

The ghostly story of the man who built the first theater in California should not be overlooked in this collection of tales. Jack Swan, a sailor by trade, arrived in Monterey in 1843. Liking what he saw, he decided to stay. In the summer of 1844 he started construction of his building. Today the "house that Jack built" is known as California's First Theater. It is on the corner of Pacific and Scott streets.

First used as a saloon and boarding house for sailors, the structure got its start as a theater in the late 1840s (or possibly 1850). The facility has also served several other functions, including being the headquarters for one of Monterey's early whaling companies. Theatrical performances of early melodramas returned there in 1937 and have been held at the site ever since.

Of interest to ghost buffs are the stories shared by the people who work around the building and take part in its productions. Several of these individuals have told me that when things are not going as they should, the ghost of Jack Swan can be seen scurrying about the halls and peering from the wings backstage!*

---

*For more ghostly happenings at California's First Theater, see the account entitled "His ghost scurries about the halls . . ." in *Ghost Notes*.

28

Numerous other buildings and oft-neglected sites boast legends of interest to both visitors and residents of old Monterey. Examples include the Jesus Soto Adobe, known to old-timers as a building with a haunted past (it has even been reported that in 1944 author John Steinbeck had the building exorcised before he moved in); the Sherman Rose Adobe and its romantic link to early California; the renowned pearls of Loreto, lost in the waters of Monterey Bay; stories of "necktie parties" at the old stone jail, including the lynching of California badman Anastacio Garcia; the once-popular Washington Hotel and its history of barroom murders; the fabulous Hotel Del Monte (now the United States Naval Postgraduate School) and its mysterious Man in Gray; and the ghosts that are said to haunt colorful Cannery Row. Those who seek them out can find countless stories that add more than a touch of mystery to the history of California's first capital city.

Chapter Four

Pacific Grove

The Monterey Peninsula's second oldest city is Pacific Grove. Founded in 1875, this charming community has been known for many things over the years, including its "puritan" origins (it was originally a Seaside Methodist Retreat), its monarch butterflies (thousands know it as "Butterfly Town U.S.A."), and the fact that it was the last "dry" town in California (Pacific Grove did not allow the sale of alcohol until 1969). Yet as important as these claims to fame are, its most recent title of "the last home town" is the one many of its residents like best.

Certainly, many reasons could be given for this title, among them the friendliness of the people, the community spirit, and the pride families take in their neighborhoods. To a newcomer, however, perhaps it is the Victorian homes found throughout the community that most evoke the "home town" feeling. Many of these aged edifices have been lovingly restored, and people from far and near come to see them. In fact, these houses are so admired that Pacific Grove's annual Victorian Home Tour is one of the community's most popular events.

The Grove's numerous Victorians boast more than towers and turrets, gingerbread trim, and interiors filled with antiques.

Several are also known for the ghostly spirits that are said to lurk in them. Tales of mysterious voices, creaky noises, and peculiar happenings are told by a surprising number of people who have lived in these dwellings.

One individual, previously a scoffer at ghostly tales, recently packed his belongings and moved from his Pacific Grove home. After settling in a nearby community, he reported a number of odd occurrences that had taken place at his Grove house, including muted voices and muffled noises coming from the closets that prevented him from sleeping. Needless to say, this former skeptic is now a firm believer in ghostly spirits and strange happenings.

Equally disturbing and mysterious incidents are reported to take place in an aged structure near the heart of the city. Perhaps of most interest to readers of this work is the description of a man's face that stares, blankly, from a wall. The apparition has been seen on numerous occasions and has been reported by several people.

One Pacific Grove home boasts a unique problem that has its owners a bit shaken. Before retiring for the night the residents of the house check to be sure that all is in order. Upon awakening the following morning they are often quite shocked to find the walls stripped of pictures, which are then found lying face down on the floor! The pictures and frames are always found to be intact, and they appear to have been placed in a particular order. Nothing else is disturbed, except for an occasional curtain being open, and all of the doors and windows are still securely locked.

The owners of a dwelling near the sea bemoan the fact that they can't keep it rented. Time after time the building's occupants pack their belongings—sometimes in the dead of night—and take their leave. More often than not their reasons for vacating the premises include "strange sounds and creepy feelings" that abound within the structure.

... ghostly blankets of drifting fog and the mournful cry
of ocean winds encouraged the spirits of this early
Pacific Grove graveyard ...

The residents of a second dwelling by the bay swear that the ghost of a long-dead sea captain paces to and fro on the front veranda, as if it were the bridge of a ship. Occasionally, they say, he stops and peers toward the fog-shrouded shore.

Speaking of ghostly happenings near the water, a brief account concerning the Pacific Grove cemetery fits in nicely here. Stories of peculiar goings-on at the graveyard date back far beyond the half-century mark, but it wasn't until World War II—when troops stationed directly across the street from the cemetery insisted on standing guard duty in pairs—that the accounts took on added meaning. Perhaps, as some surmise, phantom spirits from the graveyard, encouraged by ghostly blankets of drifting fog and the mournful cry of ocean winds, spooked the soldiers to such an extent it took two to guard against the enemy on Pacific Grove's Point of Pines.

Interestingly, a second tale of World War II is also connected with the Grove's Point Pinos. Within a stone's throw of the cemetery is the most historic lighthouse on the western seaboard. Completed in 1855, the structure is the oldest continuously operating lighthouse on the Pacific Coast. Other than boasting a ghost (thought to be the spirit of a long-dead lightkeeper), the lighthouse is noteworthy because its lens is said to have been shot at by the deck crew of a Japanese submarine. Adding to the credibility of this story, which was related to locals by a past lightkeeper, Japanese submarines *were* in the area. In fact, aged newspapers tell how a fully loaded American tanker was attacked by such a craft within sight of the Pacific Grove shore! The encounter took place on December 20, 1941, and was witnessed by many residents, including golfers on the famous Cypress Point Golf Course. After successfully outrunning their Pacific foe, the tanker's crew spent a long and restless night in the confines of Monterey Bay.

Another interesting tale connected with the Pacific Grove shore revolves around a second cemetery. This graveyard was part of a Chinese fishing village that was located on Point Cabrillo. (Point Cabrillo has also been referred to as China Point and Mussel Point. Stanford University's Hopkins Marine Station and part of the Monterey Bay Aquarium are now located on the village site.)

In the late 1800s the village was well-known throughout California. In fact, an 1888 report from the United States Commission of Fish and Fisheries went so far as to describe it as "one of the most thriving settlements of its kind on the West Coast." Many of the people who settled at the site were drifters from the Gold Country and participants in California's boom years of railroad building.

Although the account I am about to tell is not ghostly, it does concern the invisible world beyond the grave. Of special interest to me are the elaborate preparations the Chinese took to ensure a safe journey for the soul of a departed loved one to his or her final resting place in the "flowery kingdom." In their efforts to help a troubled spirit, they placed a roasted pig and an appetizing assortment of Oriental delicacies near the grave to help mitigate the spirit's appetite as it meandered toward the Chinese "Seventh Heaven." Also provided was a chair to sit on when the journey proved tiring, as well as a stove to warm ghostly hands over when the fog was thick and the way unclear.

Among other spectacles that added an Oriental influence to this bayside cemetery were hundreds of tiny red papers. Each paper had a hole in its center through which the "Honorable Devil," and all of his devilish helpers, were forced to pass before they could interfere with the upward progress of the wandering soul. Other sights and sounds that were foreign to many Pacific Grovians included burning punks, waxed decorations, fluttering red rags, and salvos of firecrackers that celebrated the start of the soul's journey to join its ancestors.

In bringing this section to a close, I should add that it was more than the activities associated with the cemetery that made Pacific Grove's Chinese fishing village a valued part of the community's past. With such things as a sampan fishing fleet, an elaborate joss house, intriguing opium dens, colorful dragon parades, noisy New Year's celebrations, mysterious alleyways, driftwood shanties, and an abundance of kind and hard-working inhabitants, it is easy to see why many local residents believe that the Monterey Peninsula lost much more than a "foul smelling eyesore" (as it was described by some) when the "great China fire" of 1906 destroyed the picturesque Chinese fishing village on the Pacific Grove shore.

Author's Note

Those who desire to learn more about Pacific Grove ghosts (particularly those that haunt its prized Victorians) may wish to consult ***Ghostly Tales and Mysterious Happenings of Old Monterey*** and ***Ghost Notes***. *In addition to ghostly accounts, these books include tales of unusual happenings associated with the sea and with seaside dwellings.*

I might add a point of interest here about the Chinese village that once overlooked Monterey Bay. The fire that destroyed the village occurred less than six weeks after the famous San Francisco earthquake and fire of 1906. The destruction of the Pacific Grove settlement was all the more tragic because a number of Chinese had taken refuge there after losing their homes in San Francisco.

In regard to the Chinese cemetery, I should note that sources differ with respect to some details. But of one thing I can be sure, and that is that even though Pacific Grove's Chinese village is long gone, it will continue to be remembered for its colorful contribution to the Monterey Peninsula's unique past.

Chapter Five

Pebble Beach

Between the communities of Pacific Grove and Carmel, and bordering much of the Monterey Peninsula's scenic southwest shore, is beautiful Pebble Beach. Although it is best known for its spectacular coastline, its wind-swept cypress trees, its magnificent mansions, and its world-famous golf courses, the Pebble Beach area also boasts other items of interest. Among them are the memories of ships that were wrecked there and the sightings of a mysterious Lady in Lace who frequents picturesque Pescadero Point.

On the subject of shipwrecks, the best-known vessel to have come to grief on the Pebble Beach shore is the *Roderick Dhu*. Fog was to blame for the mishap, which took place in the Asilomar/Spanish Bay area. Although the craft was serving as an oil barge at the time of its stranding, the record-setting ship was known to those with an interest in maritime history as "The Masterpiece of 1873."

Built in Sunderland, England, in that long-ago year, the *Roderick Dhu* was described as an "iron-hulled medium clipper." Built for speed as well as service, this remarkable craft set a number of speed records during her career. One such record is talked about to this day. That memorable voyage took place in

37

1880, when she sailed from Liverpool, England, to Calcutta, India, in just eighty-eight days!

Her first trip to California was also something special. Taking part in a race from Liverpool to San Francisco, the *Roderick Dhu* beat the second-place ship by eleven days, with the third-place vessel not arriving until three weeks later!

Becoming one of the first seven ships of the renowned Matson fleet (of Hawaiian sugar fame), the Masterpiece of '73 continued to set records and became the first sailing vessel to boast electricity and a cold storage plant.

Accomplishments like these brought honor and glory to the gallant ship. When destiny called on April 26, 1909, many of those who knew her history came to pay their respects. Over the years a number of the ship's admirers sadly watched as she was gradually pounded to pieces by the Pacific.

Interestingly, even though more than three quarters of a century have passed since the *Roderick Dhu* was wrecked, those who know where to look can sometimes still find pieces of the once-proud ship. To this day pockets of rust and bits of steel continue to mark her final resting place.*

In reference to the Lady in Lace of Pescadero Point, both residents and visitors have reported seeing the willowy figure of a lady dressed in "flowing robes of lacy white" walking down the middle of the road. Like most of the shipwrecks, the incidents involving this apparition usually took place on foggy nights. To observers, the ghostly figure appeared to be intently following the line marking the center of the scenic Seventeen Mile Drive . . . perhaps using it as a guide to help find her way.

---

*Among the other vessels of one hundred tons or larger that have met their end in the rock-bound waters of Pebble Beach are the *St. Paul* (1896), the *Celia* (1906), the *Flavel* (1923), and the *J. B. Stetson* (1934). For information regarding these and other wrecks, see my *Shipwrecks and Sea Monsters of California's Central Coast* book. And for a fascinating account of a ghostly galleon foundering on the Pebble Beach shore, see "He glimpsed a ghostly galleon . . ." in *Ghost Notes*.

. . . both residents and visitors have reported seeing the willowy figure of a lady dressed in "flowing robes of lacy white" walking down the middle of the road.

(Internationally known for its beautiful scenery and majestic vistas, the Seventeen Mile Drive winds through much of the Monterey Peninsula's Pebble Beach and Del Monte Forest areas.) Many a motorist over the years has reportedly been forced to take evasive action after suddenly coming upon the white-clad figure in the center of the road.

Also in the neighborhood of Pescadero Point is the famous ghost tree. For years this grotesquely shaped cypress tree was a landmark on the Seventeen Mile Drive. Today only part of the tree is still standing. It is near this tree that the Lady in Lace has most often been seen.

Peninsulans can only guess who the Lady in Lace might be. Some wonder whether the ghostly image is that of Dona Maria del Carmen Barreto, who sold the surrounding property in the 1840s.*

Another ghost story linked to the Pescadero Point area involves a castle-like home perched on its shore. On special occasions when parties are being given at the elegant estate, a ghostly apparition is sometimes seen on the front veranda. It is said that the dignified gentleman mingles with the unsuspecting guests, enjoying the festivities and always sporting the proper attire!

No one knows who the spirit might be. If you're lucky enough to meet the right people, perhaps the next time you visit Pebble Beach you will be invited to a gathering at their palatial home. If the dwelling is near the ghost tree, and if it boasts gold-plated bathroom fixtures (complemented by a jeweled bath mat), a beautiful swimming pool nestled in the rocks overlooking the Pacific, and striking Italian marble columns lining its entry-way, you'll know you're at the right place. As you enjoy the view from the veranda, keep a sharp eye open for a dignified gentle-man with a "haunting look." Chances are he will be the ghostly guest who—for reasons unknown—chooses to partake in the parties at this magnificent Pescadero Point home.

Numerous other mansions are found throughout Pebble Beach, and a surprising number of them boast colorful histories and haunted happenings. Sadly, one such structure has burned to the ground since I wrote about it when this book was first published. Nevertheless, even though the dwelling is no longer with us, its history is still very much a part of old Pebble Beach.

Built in 1917 by A. Kingsley Macomber, the mansion boasted massive rooms and many fireplaces (the largest of which had an opening eight feet wide and twelve feet high). The living room alone was as big as many homes, measuring more than 1,750 square feet. The unique cube-shaped dining room meas-

---

*For more information regarding the Dona Maria del Carmen Barreto theory, see "The Lady in Lace of Pebble Beach . . ." in *Ghost Notes*.

ured thirty feet in length, thirty feet in width, and an amazing thirty feet in height! Interestingly, even though the building was of gigantic proportions, it was built almost entirely of logs.

When the Macombers moved into their cavernous "log cabin," they stayed just long enough to give an elaborate dress ball for the high-society set. When the ball was over, so was the Macombers' stay! For forty years the Monterey pine mansion sat vacant. Occasionally vandals paid it a call, and it is they who are blamed for relieving its wine cellar of a valuable collection of vintage French wines during Prohibition times. A caretaker was paid to watch over the grounds (which included seventy-five acres of prime Pebble Beach property), but otherwise the edifice was left to the elements . . . and to a number of ghosts who are said to have lurked about.

Because many Peninsulans supposedly knew about the building's ghosts—with some even speculating that they were the reason the Macombers left—the structure became known as the Mystery House. However, even though the abandoned mansion was mysterious, I was unable to track down any ghostly happenings that took place there until after the building succumbed to fire in 1977. I then learned that in the late 1960s a prominent Pebble Beach couple (whose roots dated back to the area's earliest days) moved into the structure and made many changes. One day while the lady of the house was alone in one section of it, she heard a feminine voice exclaim, "Oh, dear!" The words were very distinct and came from a room the couple had converted to a small bedroom. Quickly peering into the room, the bewildered lady found it empty. She could only surmise that the unseen ghost was voicing its dismay at the changes that had been made.

I describe another ghostly incident that took place in a Pebble Beach mansion in *Ghostly Tales and Mysterious Happenings of Old Monterey*. This building resembled an elaborate Spanish villa. Perched on a hill overlooking Carmel Bay, the aged edifice was three stories high. In addition to its red tile roof and beautiful view, it is also said to have boasted a pair of elevators installed by an eccentric lady who lived there for many years. (The lady was also an invalid.)

Not to take away from the *Ghostly Tales* account, I will just mention that, like the Macomber house, this dwelling sat vacant for many years (perhaps as long as a quarter of a century) after its elderly occupant died. During this time the structure deteriorated, and its utilities were said to be turned off. It was the absence of electricity that mystified several people who reportedly heard the elevators move from floor to floor within the structure! Sadly, no further investigation is possible, inasmuch as this hillside house has since been torn down.

In closing this section I wish to report that the occupants of a fourth Pebble Beach home are not shy about describing the repeated visitations they have experienced from a past owner of the house. Their ghostly visitor has a habit of suddenly appearing and demanding that certain changes be made to various rooms. To please the disgruntled spirit, the current occupants usually make the changes, at which time the presence appears satisfied and departs . . . only to reappear at a later date with demands for additional "improvements."

The owners have resolved several times to move, but they *do* like the house. Besides, they freely admit, "Most of the changes are for the best!"

Chapter Six

Carmel Hill

Bordering part of Pebble Beach, and situated between Monterey and Carmel, is an area many Peninsulans refer to as Carmel Hill. Tales about this area date back to ancient times (as far as local history is concerned), as in 1771 Father Junipero Serra moved his mission over this hill (and away from Monterey) to a location near the mouth of a beautiful valley. Today this valley and the river that runs through it (as well as the bay the river empties into) boast the name Carmel. So too do the mission Serra started there and the village that grew up nearby more than a century later.

In the early days (long before the village got its start) the Indians and the Spanish made frequent trips over the hill, passing through a thick pine forest as they went. Old-timers claim that this forest harbored witches and ghosts, as well as assorted other creatures.

When we trace these stories back to their beginnings, we find that it was the Indians who first reported mysterious beings lurking in the trees. Just what these beings were we may never know. However, it has been suggested that it was the "civilized" pueblo of Monterey—with its gay fiestas and flowing wine—that helped to bring forth the hairy monsters and ghostly

43

figures. Certainly, it wasn't only Indians who saw the phantom spirits. Whether it was wine or something else that brought forth the images, we know that a swale—where the hilltop trail wound through a dense growth of Monterey pine—was known to locals as *El Lugar de las Brujas* (The Place of the Witches).

In other early tales, Carmel Hill's summit has been referred to as *El Cado del Diablo* (The Devil's Elbow). These stories go on to tell of a small haunted hollow atop the ridge where "fog ghosts were often seen."

It has also been stated that the spirits of *La Gallina y Gallinitos* (The Hen and Little Chickens) lurk at the top of this hill. According to an old Monterey legend, the story of *La Gallina y Gallinitos* was "whispered about the length of Alta California," and "the blackest luck would befall the person who saw *La Gallina*, or heard the plaintive cheeping of *Las Gallinitos*."

In continuing, the tale tells of a respected padre who was followed to the Carmel Hill trail by a *mal hombre* (bad man). This man coveted the sack the padre was carrying, which contained a hen and seven chicks that were destined for a sick man in Monterey.

Attacking the padre while he was on the trail, the villain hit him over the head with the butt of his pistol. Snatching the sack, the bandit continued along the trail to his house. Upon reaching his cabin he was astonished to find the sack empty. Quickly retracing his steps, he found the body of the padre. Scratching in the ground nearby were the hen and her seven chicks!

Again gathering his booty he returned to his house, only to find the sack empty upon his arrival! Once more retracing his steps, the baffled—and frightened—robber again found the chickens scratching industriously in the ground near the padre.

Glancing fearfully at the body of the holy man, the *mal hombre* is said to have put his pistol to his head and committed suicide!

44

Picking up the infant, the couple rejoiced at their good fortune—only to have the whimpering child turn into a laughing, squirming red devil!

Another story tells of a childless couple who were returning from a dance in Monterey. Upon reaching the summit of Carmel Hill, they suddenly saw a small child crying beside the dusty wagon trail. Picking up the infant, the couple rejoiced at their good fortune—only to have the whimpering child turn into a laughing, squirming red devil!

Dropping the fiendish creature, the terrified couple fled from the spot. Never again, the story concludes, did they miss mass at Monterey's Royal Presidio Chapel.

Interestingly, after this book was first published I ran across a somewhat similar Carmel Hill account. This tale is credited to the famed Carmel poet Robinson Jeffers. According to his story, many years ago two Spanish cowboys set out from Monterey for a trip to Big Sur. Upon reaching the top of Carmel Hill they heard

45

a child crying in the nearby trees. Following the sounds, they found an abandoned baby. But when they picked up the infant to see if they could be of help, "a spout of fire poured from its mouth"! The terrified cowboys threw the baby down and raced from the scene.*

In the vicinity of Carmel Hill is an area known as Jacks Peak, which was named after David Jacks, an influential resident of old Monterey. A relatively recent story about this wooded region tells of a local security officer who came upon two teenage boys who were camping on private property. As the officer approached the boys, he observed them frantically throwing their things in the back of their car.

Telling the lads to slow down and relax, the officer jokingly added, "Just because it's private property and you will have to leave, there's no need to be in that big of a hurry!"

Without so much as looking up, the teenagers continued to load the car at a furious pace. "Man, we're not leaving because of you," they told the officer. "We're getting out of here because this place is spooked!"

As they finished their packing, the youths told of hearing strange sounds, muffled conversations, breaking branches, and rustling leaves, all coming from the wooded area nearby. Their repeated investigations failed to turn up any clue about the source of the noises. But it was when their car began to gently rock "as if it were being moved by an invisible hand" that the frightened pair decided there must be better places to camp in the hills of Monterey!

Author's Note

With all the mentions of trees in this chapter (as well as in the one on Pebble Beach), it is of interest to note that the famed

---

*For a more detailed account of this tale, see "A spout of fire poured from its mouth . . ." in *Ghost Notes*. A similar story, but one that did not necessarily take place on Carmel Hill, is related in "The rider was terrified to see fang-like teeth . . .", also in *Ghost Notes*.

*author Robert Louis Stevenson was also affected by the Penin-
sula's forests and the picturesqueness of its trees when he lived
in Monterey in 1879. Appropriately enough, he likened the
hauntingly beautiful cypress trees to "ghosts fleeing before the
wind."*

Chapter Seven

Carmel-by-the-Sea

Along with its crooked streets, quaint cottages, and sandy beach, the village of Carmel-by-the-Sea boasts a sizable collection of ghost stories and mysterious happenings. Many of the strange tales are about events that have taken place at historic Carmel Mission (more formally known as *Mission San Carlos Borromeo del Rio Carmelo,* the Mission of St. Charles Borromeo of the Carmel River).

One account that has intrigued history buffs for many years was first related by long-ago hunters and campers, together with a one-time caretaker of the crumbling church ruins. (The mission church has since been restored.) It was these people who told of being awakened in the dead of night by the sounds of approaching hoofbeats. According to the tales, at such times the startled observers would glimpse a mighty white stallion bearing an unidentified horseman. Galloping through the crumbling walls of the ancient mission, and toward the foothills of the nearby Santa Lucia Mountains, the white-clad rider and his gallant mount always appeared to be in a hurry, and were always headed in a southerly direction.

More than one Peninsulan has suggested that the phantom horseman may have been a member of the Spanish expedition

Galloping through the crumbling walls of the ancient mission . . . the white-clad rider and his gallant mount always appeared to be in a hurry, and were always headed in a southerly direction.

led by the famous explorer Gaspar de Portola. Portola, as history books tell us, marched up and down the Alta California coast in 1769 in search of Monterey Bay. Although he failed to find the peaceful harbor described so eloquently by Sebastian Vizcaino more than a century and a half before, Portola did find Carmel Bay and made camp on or near its shore. Inasmuch as Portola's expedition stayed nearly two weeks in the vicinity of the present-day Carmel Mission, supporters of this theory have some interesting information to back up their beliefs. (Incidentally, Portola did locate Monterey Bay in a second expedition the following year.)

While the preceding account of the expert rider and his spirited steed is one of the most popular ghost stories connected with the mission, it is only one of many legends that circulate about the aged church. Tales of long-lost silver mines (complete with tunnels leading from the sanctuary), lost church artifacts, bandit hideouts, buried treasure, fog-like "people," and mysterious burning candles are among the many other accounts that add to the colorful heritage of California's most famous mission.*

Closer to the beach, and a pleasant walk from the mission, is a Carmel location that evoked a feeling of despair for at least two Carmelites. This account was related by an elderly lady who had lived in the village for many years. As is the custom of many of the town's residents, she was in the habit of taking long, leisurely strolls through the community. As dusk fell one evening, she was walking along a tree-lined street near the shore when she experienced a "difficult-to-describe feeling of evil." Hastening her pace, she felt the uncomfortable feeling gradually diminish once she had passed a large tree by the side of the road.

Disturbed and baffled by the evil sensation, the woman described her experience to a gentleman friend—only to discover that he, too, had experienced the same feeling, at the same time of day, in exactly the same location!

Deciding to investigate, the couple checked into the history of the area in question. As you can imagine, they were quite shaken when they learned that near the tree where they felt the evil sensations a young girl had once been murdered!

---

*These and other incidents relating to Carmel Mission can be found in *Ghostly Tales and Mysterious Happenings of Old Monterey, Ghost Notes,* and *Tales, Treasures and Pirates of Old Monterey.*

51

Not far from the site of this tragic event is a house where a well-known writer once lived. This gentleman is best remembered for his muckraking style of journalism. Because of the fame he gained from his writing, he was visited by many literary figures of his day, including Ernest Hemingway, Alice B. Toklas, Sinclair Lewis, Gertrude Stein, and John Steinbeck. Over the years more than one ghostly image is said to have been seen in the house, with the figure of John Steinbeck being one of them. (Interestingly, rumors indicate that Steinbeck may have lived in the dwelling for a short period of time.) However, more detailed sightings have been made by various people at different times of a ghost that resembles the muckracking writer who lived there for so many years.[*]

Other accounts linked to the Carmel area include tales of huge black bears in the outlying woods, aged Spanish swords being found in the sand, and a sighting of the famed evangelist Aimee Semple McPherson *after* her mysterious disappearance in southern California. Together with stories of early-day bohemians gathering on the community's picturesque beach (including such noted authors as George Sterling, Jack London, Jimmy Hopper, and Mary Austin), tales like these only add to the special mystique of Carmel-by-the-Sea.

Author's Note

*Carmel of old boasts more than its share of happenings involving famous people. To take just one example, the rugged rock house of renowned poet Robinson Jeffers, along with his work dealing with the Santa Lucia Mountains and the awesome Big Sur coast, have inspired a collection of legends and lore all their own. Some of this lore is touched on in **Ghost Notes** (see*

---

[*]For more information regarding this residence, and a sighting of the ghost that is most often seen there, see "The presence had a smirk on its face . . ." in *Ghost Notes.*

52

"A potpourri of ghosts . . ." and "Approximately twenty years after the poet's death . . ."). Carmel of more recent vintage also has its share of famous people residing in its midst. Many of the properties these people own boast their own collections of intriguing tales. One example is film star Clint Eastwood's Mission Ranch. Among the attractions that draw people to this complex are a popular Peninsula restaurant, several attractive cottages, a restored Victorian ranch house (which serves as a bed-and-breakfast inn), a number of tennis courts, and outstanding views of Carmel Bay, Point Lobos, and the Santa Lucia Mountains. Of interest to us here is the added information that the establishment also boasts colorful accounts of lost treasures (some of which are linked to nearby Carmel Mission), as well as a ghost story about the famed California bandit Joaquin Murrieta that will be touched upon in Chapter Twelve (also see "The ghost of Joaquin Murrieta . . ." in **Ghost Notes**).

Chapter Eight

Point Lobos and Carmel Highlands

On the southwest shore of Carmel Bay is the Point Lobos Reserve. The wild water and cypress-studded cliffs of this rocky headland have caused it to be described as "The Greatest Meeting of Land and Water in the World." Not only is the promontory beautiful to look at, but its history includes such things as shore whaling, abalone canning, lost (and found) treasures, Chinese smuggling, Indian gold, and long-ago shipwrecks.*

From talking to old-timers it seems that the following story is one of the most popular of the many Point Lobos tales. A very long time ago, the story goes, a Spanish ship was wrecked on the promontory. Three survivors somehow managed to reach shore, each burdened with a portion of the ship's gold.

After carefully sighting through the crotch of a cypress tree, the fortunate seafarers buried the treasure where a gnarled limb pointed.

---

*Some of this history can be found in *Ghostly Tales and Mysterious Happenings of Old Monterey; Incredible Ghosts of the Big Sur Coast; Tales, Treasures and Pirates of Old Monterey;* and *Shipwrecks and Sea Monsters of California's Central Coast.*

Making their way into Monterey, they proceeded to celebrate their good fortune. However, it wasn't long before the free-flowing whiskey at one of the local cantinas loosened the tongue of one of the survivors. Before his companions realized what was taking place, he began bragging about the buried gold. In the fight that followed, two of the sailors were killed. The third mysteriously disappeared.

Many years later an Indian working as a whaler at Whalers Cove (which is part of the Point Lobos Reserve) told of finding the long-lost treasure. After many months of searching, he reported, he had located the cypress tree that the seafarers had sighted through. Peering through the fork of the tree, he saw the remains of a gnarled limb that pointed to the ground.

Under the cover of darkness he returned to the spot and began digging. Just as his shovel hit something metallic, a strange light appeared over the point and through the trees!

Frightened by the light, the Indian immediately filled in the hole and vowed never to return—or to reveal the hiding place to anyone else.

What caused the mysterious light is anyone's guess, but, regardless of what the gold may have been worth, the superstitious Indian was convinced it wasn't worth angering the spirits of *Punta de los Lobos Marinos* (Point of the Sea Wolves)!

In addition to mysterious lights, mystifying *sounds* have recently become part of the lore of Point Lobos. In August and September of 1994 several newspapers, as well as radio and television stations, reported a series of strange underwater sounds that were being detected in the Point Lobos area. (So many news-gathering services sent representatives to the area on September 1, 1994, that the scene was described as a "media circus.")

The sounds were first reported by divers, who heard the noises at about the ninety-foot level near the entrance of Whalers Cove. Several local agencies and institutions were consulted, including the United States Naval Postgraduate School (headquar-

Just as his shovel hit something metallic, a strange light appeared over the point and through the trees!

tered in Monterey), the Monterey Bay National Marine Sanctuary, the Monterey Bay Aquarium Research Institute, and the Monterey Bay Aquarium.

As the days went by and the sounds continued to be heard (and recorded), several scientists (including experts in the field of underwater acoustics), electrical engineers, naval officers, sonarmen, Naval Postgraduate School professors, and professional divers scratched their heads and offered various theories as to what could be causing the sounds.

Some thought the source was mechanical in nature and was associated with a ship some distance away, perhaps even over the horizon. Others wondered whether commercial fishermen were to blame, suggesting that they might be creating the noises in an attempt to keep sea lions away from their catches. Such things as submarines and underwater beacons were also considered, but were just as quickly ruled out by those in the know.

Those who thought the sounds were biological also ventured several guesses. Some blamed the noises on a species of fish called midshipmen. It seems that male fish of this species emit a low-frequency mating call that has puzzled scientists in other areas (including California's bayside community of Sausalito). Another fish that had a finger pointed to it is the male grouper (which can grow to the size of a cow!). This fellow is also said to generate low-frequency sounds that can be quite loud.

Even though a handful of these theories have backers, there are those with equally impressive credentials who discount them. Given this uncertainty, it is interesting to note that the noise has been described as "a massive heartbeat-like thumping sound." Considering the fact that a huge submarine canyon runs out of Carmel Bay and past Point Lobos (to join the even larger Monterey Submarine Canyon, discussed in Chapter Ten), I can't help but wonder whether the "massive heartbeat" might have been generated by a mammoth sea beast that followed the canyon to its source (perhaps in search of food) and decided to stick around for a while to see what life was like in Carmel Bay.

Lest this explanation sound a bit bizarre, I might add that at least one creature of immense size is said to have found its way into Carmel Bay. The beast was seen by several people near the mouth of the Carmel River in 1948. Creating quite a stir when it was spotted, the odd creature lolled in the surf for a spell and became something of a celebrity along the Carmel coast.*

Finally, in discussing underwater sounds in the vicinity of Point Lobos, I should mention the muffled sounds of a sea bell that mariners of old heard in the area. The sounds remained a mystery to many until an aged and bewhiskered sea captain traced them to a ship that had sunk there many years before. While this solved the mystery for some, a more perplexing mystery was presented when the aged captain took his own life aboard the sunken craft.**

Bordering Point Lobos to the south is Carmel Highlands. This scenic cliff-side community has frequently been referred to as California's Brigadoon.

Accounts of buccaneers and bootleggers are only part of the area's colorful history, as is a tragic tale of Chinese miners who lost their lives in California's first coal mine. Beginning operation shortly after the Civil War, the mine was worked off and on until near the turn of the century. (Those who obtain permission from the property owners can still view numerous relics at the old mine site.)

During the 1880s a corporation called the Carmelo Land and Coal Company was formed. It was this organization that built new roads from the mine to coal-loading chutes at Whalers Cove. Plans for a narrow-gauge railroad were also drawn up. Before these plans could be implemented, however, two major

---

*For more information about this Carmel Bay beast, see my book *Mysterious Sea Monsters of California's Central Coast.*
**To learn more about this eerie tale, see *Ghostly Tales and Mysterious Happenings of Old Monterey* and *Incredible Ghosts of the Big Sur Coast.*

catastrophes—one following the other—resulted in the closing of the Carmel Highlands mine.

The first accident occurred at Whalers Cove, where an explosion destroyed a ship loading coal, killing all aboard. The second disaster happened at the mine itself, where seventy Chinese miners were said to be buried alive by a massive cave-in.

Whether legend or fact, the fatal cave-in continues to be discussed among old-timers of the Highlands. Several theories exist about what caused the accident. While some see the incident as "just another cave-in," others theorize that the mining company was short of funds and triggered the slide to wipe out its debts.

A third theory traces the "accident" to a few cases of smallpox that had been discovered among the miners. According to this account, all the Chinese workers were deliberately herded into the mine. With the use of a healthy plug of dynamite, the shaft was blasted shut to prevent the disease from spreading.

Whatever the true explanation may be, the lonely, brush-covered site of California's first coal mine can be a mighty unnerving place when a blanket of low-lying fog drifts in among the coastal peaks and cries of sea lions playing in the distant surf echo through the canyons—sounding for all the world like muffled cries for help coming from the sealed entrance of the long-ago mine.

Chapter Nine

Massacre Cave and the Los Burros Mining District

In this chapter we move down the Monterey County coast, past Point Lobos and the Carmel Highlands, past Mal Paso Creek and its ghostly bells, past Palo Colorado Canyon and the clatter and clamor of a phantom wagon and its spirited team, past imposing Bixby Bridge and the antique aircraft that flies under its arch, past towering Pico Blanco and its lost world of eyeless fish and long-toothed cats, past the historic Point Sur light station and its graveyard of ships (not to mention the ghost that frequents the aged lightkeeper's house), past Big Sur and its haunted hillside inn, and on to Willow Creek and its mysterious cave of death.*

It was in 1962 that four prospectors from the San Francisco Bay Area stumbled upon the sealed entrance of a cave on the western slope of the Santa Lucia Mountains. Carefully enlarging the opening, the gold seekers discovered that the long-lost cave might better be described as a tomb—for inside were the remains of ten long-dead human beings!

---

*Accounts describing the incidents mentioned in this paragraph can be found in my previously mentioned ghost, treasure, and shipwreck books.

. . . the long-lost cave might better be described as a tomb—for inside were the remains of ten long-dead human beings!

Dumbfounded by their gruesome discovery, the prospectors wisely notified authorities. Soon the press was informed of the find, and the site was dubbed Massacre Cave. An anthropologist from one of California's leading universities, together with sheriff's deputies, the county coroner, and representatives of the media, hastened to the scene to inspect the grim remains.

After careful study nine of the skulls were identified as Indian, with the tenth being of European origin (possibly Spanish). An "educated guess" placed the deaths at about 1860—

approximately one hundred years before they were found. Adding to the grisly nature of the find, most of the skulls showed signs of having been cracked, "as if by a blunt instrument."

Speculation about who might have committed the century-old murders soon was running rampant. Thoughts of what may have happened came from several sources. One tale, which connects the cave to legends of Carmel Mission, tells of a lost gold mine that had been worked by mission Indians. As with Massacre Cave, this mine was thought to be deep in the heart of the coastal mountains.

According to this story, Spanish soldiers stationed at the Monterey Presidio stumbled across the remote mine. Forcing the Indians to continue their work, the soldiers conveniently pocketed the profits. Upon receiving orders relieving them of their California duties, the soldiers killed the Indians and sealed their bodies in the mine. In this way they hoped to keep the location of the gold a secret.

Several bits of information lend credence to this tale, perhaps the most important being that gold *has* been found in the Santa Lucia Mountains near Massacre Cave. Unfortunately, the anthropologist's estimate that the deaths took place approximately one hundred years before the discovery of the skulls doesn't fit in with this theory, since the Spanish soldiers had been relieved of their California duties long before the 1860s.

Even though the anthropologist's report put a damper on the "Spanish soldiers" theory, accounts of ghostly spirits and Indian curses (to mention only a few) continue to crop up as Massacre Cave becomes better known and more people visit the site of this chamber of death.

The mention of gold in the Santa Lucias brings to mind the many stories of strange happenings connected with the hundreds of mines that once dotted the nearby mountains. A few tales will give you an idea of the legends and lore associated with this remote region.

To get to the area of the old mines, you must follow a tortuous dirt road that leads into the coast range just south of Cape San Martin. After approximately seven and a half miles of twists and turns you will reach the heart of the little-known Los Burros Mining District. Officially formed in 1875—although mining had been going on there since the 1850s—the district bustled with activity in the late 1800s. (The best-paying mine was not even discovered until 1887.)

A mining town reminiscent of camps in California's more famous "gold country" (along the western slope of the Sierra Nevadas) sprang up on a flat in the center of the district. Old-timers still talk about this "Lost City of the Santa Lucias" and joke that it had more saloons than it did people. Today, as with many of the state's early mining camps, the Los Burros town of Manchester is only a ghost of the past.

A more modern version of Los Burros ghosts is connected with a claim that was still being worked in the 1960s. Appropriately, the mine was named The Ghost of Gold. Stories associated with this claim tell of earth-bound spirits, mysterious old automobiles, and wolf-like animals that frequented the premises. Most Los Burros visitors of the 1960s scoffed at the tales, but it would be interesting to know how many of these city-dwelling skeptics took the time to search out the facts, and to try and figure out what was causing the peculiar happenings.

Perhaps, while they were at it, they should have also tried to figure out what became of the district's first recorder of claims (who disappeared in 1889), not to mention his son (the founder of the district's Last Chance Mine), who literally followed in his father's footsteps by disappearing himself—thirty years later! Interestingly, both of these men vanished while they were hiking out of the district. Neither man was ever seen again, although the bones of the son were found ten years after his death by soldiers on maneuvers in the nearby mountains.

Other unanswered questions have circulated throughout the Los Burros Mining District for many years. However, many of

Stories associated with this claim tell of earth-bound spirits, mysterious old automobiles, and wolf-like animals that frequented the premises.

these were forgotten when the disastrous "Buckeye" forest fire of 1970 spread through the area. Sadly, a number of old miners' cabins, ore bins, and stamp mills—along with the support beams of numerous tunnels and shafts—were destroyed by the fire and by subsequent winter rains. But beneath the ravages wrought by time and the elements, the haunting mysteries of Los Burros live on.

Author's Note

*Those who have become fascinated by Massacre Cave and the Los Burros Mining District may wish to read my book **Monterey's Mother Lode** (originally published as **Gold in the Santa Lucias**). Not only does this publication tell about, and* *show pictures of, the Massacre Cave skulls, but it also contains the most complete pictorial history of the Los Burros Mining District that has ever been assembled (including before-and-after illustrations of the 1970 Buckeye fire).*

A word to those who wish to visit Los Burros: be sure to honor all "No Trespassing" signs! Also, beware of rattlesnakes, steep cliffs, black widow spiders, jagged rocks, poison oak, rusty nails, and—above all—old mines, deep shafts, and neglected tunnels. And yes, four-wheel drive vehicles are recommended during certain times of the year. Even during the best of times a rugged vehicle is suggested.

Chapter Ten

Bobo the Sea Monster

While we're still in the vicinity of the Los Burros Mining District and Massacre Cave, I might mention that it was near Cape San Martin (a promontory near the entrance of Willow Creek) that many of the objects used in the mines were unloaded from small coastal freighters. From this windswept headland the items were loaded on sled-like contraptions (as there were no roads) and hauled several steep and tortuous miles into the heart of Los Burros.

Although countless other stories could be told about this section of southern Monterey County, one of my favorites takes place slightly to the west of these locations. It was here, in the restless waters of the Pacific, that a strange and frightening sea beast was seen. Observed by numerous people over the years (primarily in the 1930s and 40s), the mystery monster was described in a variety of ways. Certainly, its most notable feature was its face, which resembled that of a giant gorilla! Creating considerable concern whenever it was sighted, the Cape San Martin creature was tagged with the name Bobo and became a "living" legend of the Big Sur coast.

The mention of Bobo, and the subject of sea monsters, brings us back to the Monterey area, for a number of monster-like

67

creatures have been spotted in the waters of Monterey Bay—including a second Bobo! Even better known than the gorilla-faced beast of Cape San Martin, the Monterey Bobo became a favorite topic of conversation among people up and down the central California coast.

The odd-looking creature was observed by many sardine fishermen—as well as people from shore—during the 1920s, 30s, and 40s. For those unfamiliar with Monterey history, during much of the 1930s and early 1940s Monterey was known as the "Sardine Capital of the World." In total tonnage it is said to have ranked third among the world's major fishing ports. On several occasions during the heyday of the sardine the mysterious beast was seen in the water above the famed Monterey trench. Described by scientists as "one of the world's largest and least studied underwater chasms," this gigantic submarine canyon drops to more than twice the depth of the Grand Canyon!

Stories of strange and seldom seen sea creatures that make their home in the "fathomless" Monterey trench add much to the nautical lore of this historic bay. Accounts of Bobo alone would fill a small book. It is these stories, related by men who have spent a lifetime fishing in local waters—and who *know* when they have seen something truly unusual—that add to the credibility of Monterey Bay's monster tales.

Some early accounts of Bobo indicated that the monster had an odd, elephant-like trunk (which it could inflate and make terrifying noises with), large reddish eyes that protruded from its head and stared with an "evil glow" about them, and small arm-like fins that beat at the air when it rose from the water, as if it was using them to help keep its balance.

These details led some skeptics to think that the "monster" may have been nothing more than an elephant seal, a creature that matched some of the descriptions and, on occasion, was spotted in Monterey Bay during the time of the Bobo sightings. However, other Bobo stories—describing such things as its snake-like body, oddly shaped tail (complete with octopus-like

*. . . it had an odd, elephant-like trunk, large reddish eyes
that protruded from its head, and small arm-like fins
that beat at the air when it rose from the water . . .*

suckers on the underside), and human-like head or face—convinced others that the creature was definitely *not* a member of
the elephant seal/sea elephant family.

Sightings of Bobo were made for more than twenty years,
primarily in Monterey Bay (although similar sightings have also
been made in Carmel Bay, which, as previously stated, boasts its
own sizable submarine canyon). The question of what the mysterious monster may have been has never been satisfactorily
answered. To this day old-timers still debate the issue, and heated
discussions among those who saw the beast when they were
young sardine fishermen can still be heard on the Monterey
wharves in the early morning, before the tourists arrive on the
scene.

Author's Note

*Since this book was originally published I have interviewed many fishermen who have seen Bobo. Some of their accounts appear in other books I have written. The greatest number of their tales are in **Mysterious Sea Monsters of California's Central Coast**. Not only does this book tell about Bobo—and a number of other monster sightings—but the revised edition (published in 1993) also discusses the Monterey Submarine Canyon and the Monterey Bay National Marine Sanctuary (established in 1992). This sanctuary is the largest refuge of its kind in the nation. As its name indicates, its focal point is Monterey Bay and its fabulous submarine canyon. Incidentally, **Mysterious Sea Monsters** also discusses (and shows a picture of) the famed Moore's Beach Monster. This creature was washed onto the rocks along the bay's north shore in 1925, proving that strange and extremely rare beasts of the deep do frequent the waters of Monterey Bay.*

Chapter Eleven

Monterey Badman Tiburcio Vasquez

In addition to tales of ghostly happenings and strange creatures of the deep, Monterey and its surrounding areas also boast an abundance of stories about bandits. In fact, the lives of two of California's most notorious outlaws are linked to the Monterey area in many ways.

The names of these two bandit chiefs are Tiburcio Vasquez and Joaquin Murrieta. This chapter briefly compares their careers before delving more deeply into the life of the Monterey-born Vasquez. The next chapter discusses Joaquin Murrieta (often described as "the King of California's horseback gangsters") and tells about his local connections.

In recounting the lives of these two desperados, I should note that, according to some modern-day historians, much of what has been written about Joaquin Murrieta (who was introduced to the world during the California Gold Rush by novelist John Rollin Ridge) is based on hearsay and speculation. For this reason several local bandit buffs think—and perhaps rightly so—that the dubious title of California's "number one badman" should be bestowed upon Monterey's Tiburcio Vasquez.

Unfortunately, it is impossible to accurately compare the lives of these two gunmen, because considerable confusion surrounds Murrieta's career. Tiburcio Vasquez stood alone—or with a small, well-organized band—but records indicate there were at least five known Gold Country outlaws with the first name of Joaquin. Many "Mother Lode massacres" were "credited" only to an elusive Mexican bandit known as Joaquin. But whether the culprit in each instance was Joaquin Ocomorena, Joaquin Valenzuela, Joaquin Carrillo, Joaquin Botilleras, or Joaquin Murrieta—all known troublemakers who frequented the Sierra foothills—history fails to tell us.

Other interesting information from Gold Rush days indicates that some Anglos were in the habit of branding almost any unknown Mexican gang leader with the name of Joaquin. Eventually a number of Mexican badmen besides the five named above were referred to as Joaquin.

In contrast with the uncertainty surrounding the better known but more controversial Joaquin Murrieta, the life of Tiburcio Vasquez is an open book. Numerous documents have been written about him, with much of the information coming from eyewitness accounts and well-preserved records.

Joaquin Murrieta was in the spotlight for a relatively short three-year period, while Vasquez—counting his ten years in and out of state prisons—basked in notoriety for twenty-plus years. In many other ways, however, Tiburcio's life parallels that of Murrieta. Both were cattle thieves, stagecoach robbers, Robin Hoods, and killers, all rolled into one. Both excelled in horsemanship and were the leaders of their own banditti. And even though each favored certain regions, both roamed throughout vast areas, striking where they were least expected.

Both outlaws were admired as well as feared, and both were protected and sheltered by their admirers. They chose similar locations in which to hide out after their daring raids (often in

72

. . . the dubious title of California's "number one bad-man" should be bestowed upon Tiburcio Vasquez.

the Cantua Canyon area of Fresno County), and both had side-kicks who were considered to be among the most heartless men in the state. Murrieta's companion and bodyguard, Manuel Garcia, alias Three-fingered Jack, was said to have tortured certain individuals for the fun of watching them die. And for a time Juan Soto, alias the Human Wildcat (labeled "the fiercest outlaw in California") was Vasquez's partner in crime. Soto was said to be so ruthless that even his own companions feared him.

Perhaps the most important similarity between Murrieta and Vasquez was their dislike and distrust of Anglos. This, more than any other characteristic, brought them closer together in the public's eye. They resented the "white man's" intrusion into their social rights, and, because of this dislike, the majority of their victims were unfortunate gringos (newcomers to the area, usually Americans). This choice of victims helped to account for their popularity among many of the Spanish-speaking people of the state.

Tiburcio Vasquez was born in Monterey in 1835. During his active years he was involved in countless crimes, ranging from the abductions of beautiful women (which seemed to be a favorite pastime) to carefully planned holdups and cruel killings (several of which were blamed on his gang).

Small in stature (less than 5' 6" in height, and 130 pounds in weight), Vasquez made up for his lack of size with a cool, analyzing mind and quick, decisive actions. Even though he died before he was forty, this Monterey badman made a name for himself not only in his own home town but among all those with an interest in the colorful bandits of the Old West.

Tiburcio's outlaw career began when he was sixteen or seventeen. Attending a Monterey fandango with the noted villain Anastacio Garcia (said to have been the cousin of Three-fingered Jack), Tiburcio watched as a fight broke out between the drunken Garcia and an American seaman. Popular Monterey constable William Hardmount was called upon to stop the disturbance. In the ensuing confusion the unfortunate constable was killed.

Garcia and Vasquez beat a hasty retreat, but a third member of their group, Jose Higuera, was caught by the angry mob and unceremoniously hanged the following morning.

This event marked Tiburcio's introduction to a life of crime. Garcia subsequently became his boon companion and proceeded to teach him the trade. Their relationship was short-lived, however, for Garcia was captured six months later and placed in the Monterey jail. The notorious outlaw met a sudden end when a mob broke into his cell and lynched him while many of the local citizens attended church services.

An unmarked grave near the entrance of Carmel Mission is said to contain Garcia's remains. Tradition states that shortly before he was hanged, he asked to be buried where the church worshippers "might ever tread" upon his grave.

While the career of Anastacio Garcia was being cut short, that of Tiburcio Vasquez was only beginning. He added his own unique touch to numerous robberies by taking the trouble to apologize to his victims and explain that he was merely taking a loan. He even told some of them that he would repay them with interest. Of course, this never happened, although Vasquez reportedly took pains to return stolen mounts to their rightful owners.

Encounters with pretty señoritas dot his career. In at least one case, a romantic interlude is said to have been his downfall. While running off a herd of cattle in Sonoma County, Tiburcio urged his companions to proceed without him when a rancher's pretty daughter caught his eye. Dallying too long with this north state beauty, he was subsequently caught and sent to San Quentin.

Vasquez engaged in any number of other exploits, and many stories are told of his narrow escapes and the scars he took to the grave as proof of these encounters. One tale that bears repeating tells of a game of hide-and-seek he played with the local sheriff.

It seems that one of Tiburcio's favorite escapades was to make a daring foray into the heart of Monterey. He would then quietly slip into his sister's adobe, which was conveniently located behind the jail. Here, in the comfort of his sister's parlor, he would watch the harassed sheriff organize a posse and ride off in search of the "cunning villain."

During one such episode the sheriff was tipped off. As his men attempted to surround the house, Vasquez beat a hasty retreat—barely escaping with his life and his loot!

Probably the most publicized of Tiburcio's brushes with death tells of an authentic Wild West shootout in the hills near Santa Cruz. Even though he was severely wounded by Marshall L. T. Roberts, Vasquez managed to stand his ground and return the fire. By the time calm was restored, Roberts lay seriously wounded. Thinking that the marshall was dead, Vasquez wearily mounted his horse and rode to his Cantua Canyon hideout.

A number of incidents added to the notoriety of Vasquez and his men and brought the public's cries of "Justice!" to the attention of California's governor, Newton Booth. They included the August 26, 1873, robbery of Snyder's Store (at Tres Pinos) and the senseless killing of three people; the December 26, 1873, looting of the community of Kingston (in this bold robbery Vasquez and his gang are credited with tying up between twenty and thirty men and making a getaway without a life being lost); and, finally, the casual February 25, 1874, holdup of the Coyote Wells Stage Station.

With the rewards being upped to $6,000—DEAD and $8,000—ALIVE, Tiburcio's days as a free man were numbered.

The story of his final capture and subsequent lodging in the San Jose jail has often been told. While awaiting trail Vasquez was the picture of a perfect gentleman (some sources compare him to an elegant Mexican don). He had frequent visitors, many of them women who brought him fine food and wine, and was interviewed often by reporters from leading newspapers. As always, he dressed neatly, and he even posed for pictures.

Speaking in his own defense at his trial, Vasquez repeatedly denied ever killing a man. Several witnesses, however, disagreed. On January 23, 1875, the final verdict was read, and Tiburcio was given the death penalty. The dapper bandido paled but showed no other sign of emotion.

On March 19, 1875, Tiburcio Vasquez approached the gallows. Holding a crucifix in one hand, he calmly removed his coat, collar, and tie. A hush fell over the crowd as the priest administered the last rites. At exactly 1:35 p.m. the noose was adjusted around the condemned man's neck and the black cap shut out the world. With his last word of "Pronto!" ("Quickly!"), the trap was sprung.

The death of Vasquez marked the beginning of the end of California's horseback gangsters. Others were to follow, but none quite compared to Joaquin Murrieta or Tiburcio Vasquez.

Author's Note

If you chuckled over Tiburcio's "daring forays" into Monterey, and his subsequent hiding out in the parlor of his sister's adobe, you may wish to visit the original site at 546 Dutra Street. Those who wish to visit his grave will have to travel to the Santa Clara Mission Cemetery, near Mission Santa Clara in Santa Clara, California. The grave won't be hard to find, since, according to legend, the headstone was placed at an angle to remind passersby that he had died in disrepute.

Chapter Twelve

Joaquin Murrieta, King of California's Horseback Gangsters

As I indicated in the preceding chapter, the legendary Joaquin Murrieta had his own connections to the Monterey area. Fittingly enough, in telling his story this final chapter touches on all the themes of this book—including not only bandits and legends, but a ghost story or two besides!

Coming to California with other gold seekers from his home in Sonora, Mexico, Joaquin Murrieta and his wife settled in the Southern Mines area of California's Mother Lode region (perhaps in the vicinity of San Andreas, or one of several other nearby camps that have become part of the Murrieta legend). Like many of his countrymen, Joaquin began the task of gathering gold. However, it wasn't long before the dream of striking it rich was interrupted by a rough gang of gringos.

Overpowering Joaquin, the intruders proceeded to do as they pleased, even abusing his wife. This, coupled with a second encounter with a band of gringos that resulted in the killing of

79

. . . an enraged Joaquin vowed to get revenge on each and every gringo who had taken part in the atrocities.

his half-brother on a trumped-up charge of horse stealing, prompted Murrieta to turn to a life of crime. As he started down the outlaw trail, an enraged Joaquin vowed to get revenge on each and every gringo who had taken part in the atrocities.

Legend states that he succeeded in "evening the score" by killing the gringos in a variety of imaginative ways. By the time this grisly task was completed, word of the vengeful killings had spread throughout the Mother Lode, and Joaquin Murrieta's name was known throughout the Sierras.

As I mentioned in Chapter Eleven, it wasn't only the name of Joaquin Murrieta that brought fear to the gold seekers. At about the same time, a handful of other desperados named Joaquin were also practicing their trade in the gold fields. But because Murrieta was the best known of the Joaquins, he and his bandit gang were blamed for countless crimes they didn't commit.

During this period—when things got too hot—Murrieta and some of his followers ventured into other parts of the state. There they continued their outlaw ways. In some instances they are even described as having been chased to the outlying areas by angry miners and hastily organized posses.

It is one such tale that brings us to the Monterey Peninsula. Although there is some confusion about who his pursuers were, the account indicates that Murrieta arrived in the Monterey/Carmel area just ahead of a posse from the Santa Clara Valley. It is unclear whether the posse had trailed him all the way from the Mother Lode, or whether Joaquin had gotten into trouble in the Santa Clara Valley. In any case, Murrieta made it to the Carmel Mission, where, legend states, he was hidden by a priest. Not only did the priest give Joaquin refuge, but he is said to have painted the only true likeness of the bandit king that is known to exist.

With Murrieta having stayed at the famed Carmel church, it is only natural that stories of lost treasures and buried bonanzas would crop up. Among these is an account of a secret tunnel leading away from the mission (where Joaquin allegedly stumbled upon the remains of a silver mine that had once been worked by the padres) and a cache of octagonal gold pieces worth $75,000 that Murrieta had stolen from a mint in the Auburn area of the Mother Lode.

Such tales make for good reading, but the question of whether there is any truth to them must be asked. Interestingly, in this case the answers—at least in part—may be yes! For example, an aged passageway *has* been found leading away from the church (and toward the Victorian ranch house of neighboring Mission Ranch). Moreover, rocks containing silver *have* turned up near the mission and its mysterious tunnel-like passageway. As for the stash of octagonal gold pieces, a newspaper account printed long after Joaquin left the area indicated that approximately $10,000 worth of the treasure *had* been recovered in the vicinity of Carmel.

Even though the preceding information may have just whetted your appetite, I will leave any additional research up to you. As promised at the start of this chapter, I would like to close this book with a pair of stories that have a "ghostly" twist. For openers, let me say that according to one of these two tales, "El Famoso" (Joaquin Murrieta) *returned* to the Carmel Valley area more than twenty years after his "death"!

To appreciate this account it is important that you know the story of the alleged killing of Joaquin—and his sidekick, Three-fingered Jack—by Captain Harry S. Love and the California Rangers in 1853. As proof that they had "gotten their man," the Rangers took the head of Murrieta and the hand of Three-fingered Jack to the state capital (then in Benicia) to claim their reward.

After the reward was paid, and the governor (along with members of the state legislature) breathed a sigh of relief, rumors began to circulate throughout the Sierra foothills that the "pickled" head was *not* that of Murrieta! Regardless of the rumors, it is a fact that after the Cantua Canyon shootout (in which Love

82

and his Rangers were credited with killing the most famous of the Mother Lode marauders), crime in the Gold Country began to slack off, and the mining camps became more peaceful places in which to live.

Now that you know how Joaquin *supposedly* met his end, the following account should take on more meaning. The incident I am about to relate took place at Carmel Valley's Los Laureles Ranch in 1877. The story is taken from a document written by a pioneer Monterey County resident who was born along the Big Sur coast in 1859. Because of his eventful life, the man's family asked him to record some of his memories before he died. Contained in these reminiscences was an account about an experience he had had while working as a ranch hand at the Los Laureles Ranch.

According to his tale, when he was still a teenager he witnessed a conversation between a stranger and the ranch foreman (a fellow by the name of Kinzie Clinkenbeard). During the conversation Clinkenbeard mentioned his father's inn in the Sierras, which the stranger was familiar with. It seems that as a young man the foreman had waited on Murrieta when he and his gang had visited his father's roadhouse. Clinkenbeard then surprised the stranger by asking if *he* was Joaquin Murrieta! Even though the stranger was a bit taken aback, he acknowledged that he was. He went on to say that he had come back to the area to fetch some treasure he and his men had buried many years before!

I have reason to think that this amazing story of the "long-dead" Murrieta's reappearance in Carmel Valley is more than fiction. It is information like this (which occasionally crops up even today) that causes me to side with the Gold Country rumors in the belief that it *wasn't* Joaquin Murrieta who was killed by the California Rangers in the Cantua Canyon shootout of 1853.

In closing I will briefly return to the Mission Ranch and a tale about Murrieta's ghost. Reportedly, the presence of this dreaded desperado is sometimes seen in the bunkhouse of the aged establishment. Why the ghost of California's best-known badman would return to the Mission Ranch bunkhouse is anyone's guess. Perhaps (as I have suggested elsewhere) he is paying a social call on a certain female ghost who is also said to frequent the premises . . . and who is always attired in a gown of white.

Author's Note

Over the years there has been so much speculation about Joaquin Murrieta that it is impossible to separate fact from fiction, and much of what has been written about him should not be taken too seriously. However, we should also remember that a good part of the Murrieta story (such as the California Rangers' pursuit of this legendary figure) is based on fact. Therefore, we cannot discount all of the accounts that have been recorded about him.

This, coupled with the fact that the story of Joaquin's return to Carmel Valley, is in my opinion true, I (for one) can't help but think that many of the other Murrieta "myths" may also be based on actual events.

Finally, Monterey-area bandit buffs may be interested in knowing that one highly respected California historian—a man who spent more than half a century researching the life of Joaquin Murrieta—is of the opinion that the famed outlaw was "for real" and that the head that was passed off as his was, instead, the head of a Carmel Valley Indian who worked as a hostler for the Murrieta gang.

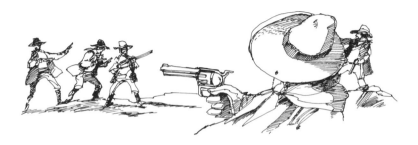

Afterword

A Word about Ghosts

As indicated in the Introduction to this book, my interest in ghostly happenings in the Monterey area began with a magazine article I wrote in 1970 called "Ghosts of Old Monterey." Now, a quarter of a century later, I would like to say that since this book was first published I have talked to countless local residents—as well as visitors to the area—who have experienced strange and unexplained happenings in and about the Monterey Peninsula. (Many of these encounters are described in my other ghost books.) When I consider the caliber of people I have talked to—including clergymen, doctors, lawyers, educators, and police officers—I am forced to admit that odd, and unusual, occurrences *do* take place! It is hardly credible that so many people could be either imagining things or deliberately making up stories.

As a final note, I want to add that, in my opinion, ghosts all too often get a bad rap. Over the years, many of those who have "felt the presence" or "experienced the supernatural" have described their encounters to me as warm and comforting, almost as if someone or something were watching over and protecting them. So, if you are one of those who associate thrills and chills with ghosts, and seek the sensational when you go ghost hunting, don't be surprised if the spirits you find are of the friendly kind and want nothing more than to welcome you to their ghostly haunts.

Books by Randall A. Reinstedt

California Ghost Notes

Regional History and Lore Series . . .
bringing the colorful history of California's Central Coast
to life for adults and older children:

Ghost Notes
Ghostly Tales and Mysterious Happenings of Old Monterey
Ghosts, Bandits and Legends of Old Monterey
Ghosts of the Big Sur Coast
Incredible Ghosts of Old Monterey's Hotel Del Monte
Monterey's Mother Lode
Mysterious Sea Monsters of California's Central Coast
Shipwrecks and Sea Monsters of California's Central Coast
Tales, Treasures and Pirates of Old Monterey
Where Have All the Sardines Gone?

History & Happenings of California Series . . .
putting the story *back in* history *for young readers:*

Lean John, California's Horseback Hero
One-Eyed Charley, the California Whip
Otters, Octopuses, and Odd Creatures of the Deep
Stagecoach Santa
The Strange Case of the Ghosts of the
    Robert Louis Stevenson House
Tales and Treasures of California's Missions
Tales and Treasures of California's Ranchos
Tales and Treasures of the California Gold Rush

For information on purchasing books contact:

Ghost Town Publications
P.O. Drawer 5998 ◆ Carmel, CA 93921 ◆ (831) 373-2885
www.ghosttownpub.com